Cambridge English

Movers 8

Answer Booklet

CAMBRIDGE
UNIVERSITY PRESS

University Printing House, Cambridge CB2 8BS, United Kingdom

Cambridge University Press is part of the University of Cambridge.

It furthers the University's mission by disseminating knowledge in the pursuit of education, learning and research at the highest international levels of excellence.

www.cambridge.org
Information on this title: www.cambridge.org/9781107690899

© Cambridge University Press 2013

First published 2013
6th printing 2015

Printed in China by Golden Cup Printing Co. Ltd

A catalogue record for this publication is available from the British Library

ISBN 978-1-107-61307-2 Student's Book
ISBN 978-1-107-69089-9 Answer Booklet
ISBN 978-1-107-61785-8 Audio CD

Cover design by Peter & Jan Simmonett
Produced by Kamae Design, Oxford

Contents

Introduction

The *Cambridge English: Young Learners* tests offer an elementary-level testing system (up to CEFR level A2) for learners of English between the ages of 7 and 12. The tests include three key levels of assessment: *Starters*, *Movers* and *Flyers*.

Movers is the second level in the system. Test instructions are very simple and consist only of words and structures specified in the syllabus.

The complete test lasts about an hour and has the following components: Listening, Reading and Writing, and Speaking.

	length	number of parts	number of questions
Listening	approx. 25 minutes	5	25
Reading and Writing	30 minutes	6	40
Speaking	approx. 5–7 minutes	4	–

Candidates need a pen or pencil for the Reading and Writing paper, and coloured pens or pencils for the Listening paper. All answers are written on the question papers.

Listening

In general, the aim is to focus on the 'here and now' and to use language in meaningful contexts. In addition to multiple-choice and short-answer questions, candidates are asked to use coloured pencils to mark their responses to one of the tasks. There are five parts. Each part begins with a clear example.

part	main skill focus	input	expected response	number of questions
1	the main skill focus in all five parts of the Listening test is listening for specific information of various kinds, e.g. numbers, describing people, etc.	picture, names and dialogue	draw lines to match names to people in a picture	5
2		form or page of notepad with missing words and dialogue	write words or numbers in gaps	5
3		pictures, days of the week and dialogue	draw lines from days of week to correct pictures	5
4		3-option multiple-choice pictures and dialogues	tick boxes under correct picture	5
5		picture and dialogue	carry out instructions to colour, draw and write (range of colours is: black, blue, brown, green, grey, orange, pink, purple, red, yellow)	5

Reading and Writing

Again, the focus is on the 'here and now' and the use of language in meaningful contexts where possible. To complete the test, candidates need a single pen or pencil of any colour. There are six parts, each starting with a clear example.

part	main skill focus	input	expected response	number of items
1	reading short definitions and matching to words writing words	labelled pictures and definitions	copy the correct words next to the definitions	6
2	reading sentences about a picture and writing one-word answers	one picture and sentences	write 'yes'/'no'	6
3	reading a dialogue and choosing the correct responses	one picture and short dialogue with multiple-choice responses	choose correct response by circling a letter	6
4	reading for specific information and gist copying words	cloze text, words and pictures	choose and copy missing words correctly; tick a box to choose the best title for the story	7
5	reading a story and completing sentences about the story	story, pictures and gapped sentences	complete sentences about the story by writing 1, 2 or 3 words	10
6	reading and understanding a factual text copying words	gapped text and 3-option multiple choice (grammatical words)	complete text by selecting the correct words and copying them in corresponding gaps	5

Speaking

In the Speaking test, the candidate speaks with one examiner for about six minutes. The format of the test is explained in advance to the child in their native language by a teacher or person familiar to them. This person then takes the child into the exam room and introduces them to the examiner.

Speaking ability is assessed according to various criteria, including comprehension, the ability to produce an appropriate response and pronunciation.

part	main skill focus	input	expected response
1	describing two pictures by using short responses	two similar pictures	identify four differences between pictures
2	understanding the beginning of a story and then continuing it based on a series of pictures	picture sequence	describe each picture in turn
3	suggesting a picture which is different and explaining why	picture sets	identify the odd one out and give reason
4	understanding and responding to personal questions	open-ended questions about candidate	answer personal questions

Further information

The topics, structures, words and tasks upon which the *Cambridge English: Young Learners* tests are based are comprehensively described in the Handbook, so teachers or parents can know exactly what to expect.

Further information about the *Cambridge English: Young Learners* tests can be obtained from the Centre Exams Manager for Cambridge ESOL examinations in your area, or from:

University of Cambridge ESOL Examinations
1 Hills Road
Cambridge
CB1 2EU
United Kingdom

Telephone: +44 1223 553997
Fax: +44 1223 553621

Email: ESOLHelpdesk@CambridgeESOL.org
www.CambridgeESOL.org

Test 1 Answers

Listening

Part 1 (5 marks)

Lines should be drawn between:

1 Sally and the girl with long hair, riding a bike
2 Vicky and the girl in the orange jacket, at the top of the tree
3 John and the man at the front of the picture, with a dog
4 Anna and the woman waving with both hands, by the waterfall
5 Bill and the man fishing on the lake

Part 2 (5 marks)

1 (it's) black　　2 (a/the) playground　　3 (her/Gill's) lunch
4 Bold (correct spelling)　　5 (class) 11/eleven

Part 3 (5 marks)

1 Tuesday – watching TV
2 Thursday – walk on beach
3 Wednesday – market, rabbit
4 Friday – library, choosing book
5 Sunday – sailing at beach

Part 4 (5 marks)

1 A　　2 B　　3 A　　4 C　　5 B

Part 5 (5 marks)

1 Colour the scarf on the stairs – purple
2 Colour the flowers in the round window – pink
3 Write 'food' under 'bird' on the box
4 Colour the parrot's tail – green
5 Colour the glass with water in it – blue

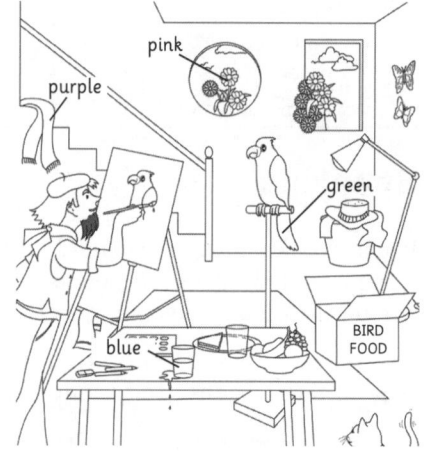

TRANSCRIPT	*Hello. This is the Cambridge Movers Practice Listening Test, Test 1.*
Part 1	*Look at Part 1. Look at the picture. Listen and look. There is one example.*
	[pause]
Boy:	Look! We took a lot of pictures on holiday in the mountains.
Woman:	Oh, show me. Are you in this picture?
Boy:	No, but my brother Paul is. Look, he's sitting on a rock and reading a comic.
Woman:	Oh, yes.
	[pause]
	Can you see the line? This is an example. Now you listen and draw lines.
	[pause]

1

Woman:	Who's the girl who's riding the bike?
Boy:	The girl with the long hair?
Woman:	Yes.
Boy:	That's Sally. She's my sister's friend.

[pause]

2

Boy:	And can you see my friend? She's wearing an orange jacket. She loves climbing!
Woman:	Yes. Wow! She's at the top of that tree!
Boy:	I know.
Woman:	And what's her name?
Boy:	It's Vicky. She's funny. I like her a lot.

[pause]

3

Woman:	And who are the people walking behind the dog? You can't see their faces.

BOY: Oh, the man's name is John. He's got curly hair like mine.
WOMAN: Oh, yes. Does he live there?
BOY: No. He and his wife were on holiday like us.

[pause]

4

BOY: And look at my mum!
WOMAN: Where's she?
BOY: It's difficult to see her. She's waving with both hands. Look, next to the waterfall.
WOMAN: Oh, yes. And what's her name?
BOY: It's Anna.

[pause]

5

WOMAN: Is that your dad who's fishing on the lake?
BOY: Yes. His name's Bill.
WOMAN: Did he catch any fish?
BOY: No, but he likes trying!

[pause]

Now listen to Part 1 again.

[The recording is repeated.]

[pause]

That is the end of Part 1.

[pause]

Part 2   *Listen and look. There is one example.*

[pause]

GIRL: Hello! Can you help me? I can't find my school bag.
MAN: Oh dear!
GIRL: Yes. I put it on the floor and now I can't find it.
MAN: OK, Jill. I must write this down ... your school bag and you lost it here.

[pause]

Can you see the answer? Now you listen and write.

[pause]

1

MAN: OK. What colour is your bag?
GIRL: It's black.
MAN: Black? And was it new?
GIRL: Yes. My grandma bought it for me last week.

[pause]

2

MAN: And where did you lose it? In the classroom?
GIRL: No. It was in the playground.

MAN: In the playground ... and it's not there now?
GIRL: No!

[pause]

3

MAN: And what was inside it?
GIRL: My lunch. That's all.
MAN: Only your lunch?
GIRL: Yes.
MAN: Not your books, or any pens and pencils?
GIRL: No. They're all on my desk.

[pause]

4

MAN: OK. Now, what's your family name, Jill?
GIRL: It's Bold.
MAN: Right! Do you spell that B-O-L-D?
GIRL: Yes, B-O-L-D.

[pause]

5

MAN: OK. Now, what class are you in?
GIRL: Class 11.
MAN: OK. Well, go back to class 11 now, Jill.
GIRL: All right, but can you find my bag, please?
MAN: Yes, I think we can, but you must be more careful with your things, Jill.
GIRL: I know!

[pause]

Now listen to Part 2 again.

[The recording is repeated.]

[pause]

That is the end of Part 2.

[pause]

Part 3   *Look at the pictures. What did Tony do last week?*

Listen and look. There is one example.

[pause]

WOMAN: Did you have a good week last week, Tony?
BOY: Yes, I did, Aunt May. On Monday, I played in the garden with Daisy.
WOMAN: Who's Daisy?
BOY: My pet rabbit. She was naughty! She ate Mum's vegetables!
WOMAN: Oh dear!

[pause]

Can you see the line from the word Monday? On Monday, Tony played with his naughty rabbit. Now you listen and draw lines.

[pause]

1

WOMAN:	Did you go out on Tuesday?
BOY:	No, it rained on Tuesday. We played games on the floor and watched TV.
WOMAN:	And what did you watch?
BOY:	A film about animals that could talk. They lived in a forest.

[pause]

2

BOY:	I enjoyed Thursday more.
WOMAN:	Why? What did you do on Thursday?
BOY:	We drove down to the beach and went for a walk there.
WOMAN:	And did you go sailing?
BOY:	No, it was too cold.

[pause]

3

BOY:	Mum and I went to the market on Wednesday.
WOMAN:	What did you buy there?
BOY:	We bought another rabbit … a friend for Daisy.
WOMAN:	Is the new rabbit naughty too?
BOY:	No! And she's got big brown and white ears. I love her.

[pause]

4

WOMAN:	What did you do on Friday?
BOY:	We went to the library to choose some new books.
WOMAN:	And did you find an exciting story to read?
BOY:	Yes. I found a story about a family who go on holiday to the beach.
WOMAN:	And what do they do there?
BOY:	They find some treasure!

[pause]

5

BOY:	And we went to the beach again on Saturday. Oh, no, it was Sunday. Sorry.
WOMAN:	Was the weather good?
BOY:	Yes. It was nice that day and we went sailing.
WOMAN:	Great!
BOY:	Yes. It was an exciting day. I enjoyed it.

[pause]

Now listen to Part 3 again.

[The recording is repeated.]

[pause]

That is the end of Part 3.

[pause]

Part 4 *Look at the pictures. Listen and look.*

There is one example.

[pause]

What's Lucy's father doing?

[pause]

GIRL:	Where's Dad, Mum? Is he cooking dinner?
WOMAN:	No, Lucy. I think he's watching a DVD.
GIRL:	But he's not in the living room.
WOMAN:	Look … he's cleaning his motorbike.
GIRL:	Oh, yes. Thanks!

[pause]

Can you see the tick? Now you listen and tick the box.

[pause]

1 Where's the new bird cage?

BOY:	Where's the new bird cage? I want to put it in my bedroom. Is it in the garden?
WOMAN:	No. It's out on the balcony, Sam. I put it there this morning.
BOY:	Can I go and get it?
WOMAN:	Yes, but carry it very carefully.

[pause]

2 How did Peter go to work today?

MAN:	Peter started work in the city today.
WOMAN:	Did he?
MAN:	Yes. He drove there in his car, but it was very slow.
WOMAN:	Oh.
MAN:	Yes. It's easier and quicker to catch a bus or go on the train.

[pause]

3 Which is Tom's favourite sport?

WOMAN:	Did you go skating again yesterday, Tom?
BOY:	No. I don't like that now. I played table tennis.
WOMAN:	And do you like table tennis best now?
BOY:	Hmm. I think basketball is better. That's my favourite.

[pause]

4 What did May buy in the shop today?

WOMAN:	I bought this new coat today in town.
MAN:	Did you, May? But you wanted a skirt! You told me this morning!
WOMAN:	I know. But I saw this and I loved it. It's grey, like my favourite sweater.
MAN:	OK.

[pause]

5 Where's Sally's grandma?

GIRL:	Where's Grandma, Dad? Did she go for a walk with the dog?

MAN: No, Sally. She went to bed because she's got a headache.
GIRL: Oh dear! Is she OK?
MAN: Oh, yes. Go and make her a cup of tea.
GIRL: All right.

[pause]

Now listen to Part 4 again.

[The recording is repeated.]

[pause]

That is the end of Part 4.

[pause]

Part 5   *Look at the picture. Listen and look.*

There is one example.

[pause]

WOMAN: Would you like to colour this picture now? Look, a man is painting.
BOY: Oh, yes! He's got a funny beard. Can I colour it?
WOMAN: Yes. Good idea! Colour his beard red, please.
BOY: All right.

[pause]

Can you see the man's red beard? This is an example. Now you listen and colour and write.

[pause]

1

WOMAN: Can you see the man's scarf – the one on the stairs?
BOY: Yes. Shall I colour that too?
WOMAN: Yes. How about purple?
BOY: That's a good colour for a scarf. OK!
WOMAN: Thanks!

[pause]

2

BOY: His room's got two windows!
WOMAN: Yes. Find the flowers in the round window.
BOY: In the round window. Oh, yes! I can see it.
WOMAN: Well done. Colour those flowers pink, please.
BOY: All right. I'm doing that now.

[pause]

3

WOMAN: Now, can you write something on this picture too?
BOY: Yes.
WOMAN: Good. Can you see the box on the floor? It's open.
BOY: Yes, it has 'BIRD' on it.
WOMAN: That's right. Please write 'FOOD' under 'BIRD'.

BOY: 'Bird food'! All right.

[pause]

4

BOY: I love the parrot. Can it talk?
WOMAN: I don't know, but let's colour its tail.
BOY: OK. How about green?
WOMAN: Hmm … yes. That's the right colour for a parrot's tail.

[pause]

5

WOMAN: Now, the glass on the table. Colour that, please.
BOY: The one with the water in it?
WOMAN: Yes. Can you colour that glass blue?
BOY: Yes. There!
WOMAN: Well done. It looks great.
BOY: Thank you.

[pause]

Now listen to Part 5 again.

[The recording is repeated.]

[pause]

That is the end of the Movers Practice Listening Test 1.

Reading and Writing

Part 1 (6 marks)

1 stars   2 fields   3 a city
4 snow   5 clouds   6 leaves

Part 2 (6 marks)

1 no   2 no   3 yes   4 yes   5 yes   6 no

Part 3 (6 marks)

1 C   2 B   3 A   4 A   5 C   6 B

Part 4 (7 marks)

1 told   2 pointed   3 paint   4 sock
5 mirror   6 stairs
7 Mary and the clown's clothes

Part 5 (10 marks)

1 dancing   2 Saturday(s)   3 Sally's (big) sister
4 (her) father/dad/daddy   5 a (new) dress
6 market   7 white   8 Lucy's (house/home)
9 Wednesday   10 a/the CD

Part 6 (5 marks)

1 eat   2 sleeping   3 every   4 them   5 do

Speaking

Part	Examiner does this:	Examiner says this:	Minimum response expected from child:	Back-up questions:
	Usher brings candidate in.	Usher to examiner: **Hello. This is (child's name)*.**		
		Examiner: **Hello, *. My name's Jane/Ms Smith.**	Hello.	
		How old are you, *?	nine	**Are you nine/ten?**
1	Points to **Find the differences** pictures.	**Look at these pictures. They look the same, but some things are different. Here there are two photos on the wall, but here there are three.**		
		What other different things can you see?	Describes four other differences: • kangaroo on/under bed • books/lamp on table • orange/purple blanket • scarf/no scarf	Point to other differences the candidate does not mention. Give first half of response: **Here the kangaroo is on the bed, but here …**
2	Points to **Picture Story**. Allows time to look at the pictures.	**Now look at these pictures. They show a story. It's called 'The naughty dolphins'. Just look at the pictures first.** **(Pause.) Look at the first one.** **Peter, Daisy and their parents are going to the zoo. The dolphins in the zoo are good at jumping and the children want to see them.** **Now you tell the story.** (pointing at the other pictures)	(Many variations possible) *The dolphins are not jumping and the children are not happy.* *Mum, Dad and the children are going now. They want to see the pandas.* *Now the dolphins are jumping. But the family are looking at the pandas and they don't see them.*	Questions to prompt other parts of the story: **Are the dolphins jumping?** **Are the children happy?** **Where are Mum, Dad and the children going?** **What are the dolphins doing now? Are the family looking at them?**

* Remember to use the child's name throughout the test.

Part	Examiner does this:	Examiner says this:	Minimum response expected from child:	Back-up questions:
3	Points to **Odd-one-out** pictures.	**Now look at these four pictures. One is different. The book is different. A lemon, a pineapple and an orange are fruit. You eat them. You don't eat a book. You read it.**		
	Points to the second, third and fourth sets of pictures in turn.	**Now you tell me about these pictures. Which one is different? (Why?)**	Candidate suggests a difference (any plausible difference is acceptable).	**These things are all … ?** (old) **And this is … ?** (new)
				What are these people doing? (swimming) **And this girl?** (fishing)
				Where are these people? (bathroom) **And this man?** (dining room)
4	Puts away all pictures.	**Now let's talk about the places you go to.**		
		Where do you go after school?	*home*	**Do you go *home*?**
		Where do you like going with your friends?	*(to the) park*	**Do you like going to the *park*?**
		Where's the best place to go at the weekend?	*cinema*	**Do you go to the *cinema*?**
		Tell me about your holidays.	*I go to the beach.* *I play with my friends.*	**Do you go to the *beach*? Do you *play with your friends*?**
		OK, thank you, *. **Goodbye.**	**Goodbye.**	

* Remember to use the child's name throughout the test.

Test 2 Answers

Listening

Part 1 (5 marks)

Lines should be drawn between:

1 Sally and the girl with her feet in the water and a towel above her head
2 Fred and the boy with a parrot on his shoulder
3 Paul and the boy playing in the sand between the rocks, making a star
4 Mary and the woman wearing a sunhat, carrying bags
5 Vicky and the girl with a drink in her hand and a dolphin on her T-shirt

Part 2 (5 marks)

1 10/ten   2 (on) Monday(s)   3 Caris (correct spelling)
4 (some) (new) shoes   5 (Daisy's/my/your/her) bike

Part 3 (5 marks)

1 Friday – a party
2 Thursday – walk in the park
3 Sunday – cinema, film about rabbits
4 Tuesday – read book in living room
5 Saturday – football and picnic in the garden

Part 4 (5 marks)

1 C   2 A   3 B   4 B   5 A

Part 5 (5 marks)

1 Colour the bigger bowl – blue
2 Colour the doll on the table – green
3 Draw a bottle in the cupboard with the open door
4 Colour the round bag – pink
5 Colour the big plant outside the window – purple

TRANSCRIPT   *Hello. This is the Cambridge Movers Practice Listening Test, Test 2.*

Part 1   *Look at Part 1. Look at the picture. Listen and look. There is one example.*

[pause]

BOY: I took this picture when I had my beach holiday. Do you like it?
WOMAN: Yes, I do. Are these people all your friends?
BOY: Some of them are. Can you see the boy with the boat? The one who's wearing jeans?
WOMAN: Yes.
BOY: Well, that's Jim. I like him a lot.

[pause]

Can you see the line? This is an example. Now you listen and draw lines.

[pause]

1

BOY: There's another friend of mine. That's Sally.
WOMAN: Which one's she?
BOY: The girl with her feet in the water.
WOMAN: I see her. She's holding a towel above her head.
BOY: Yes, that's right.

[pause]

2

WOMAN: And what about that boy there? What's he got on his shoulder?
BOY: It's a parrot.
WOMAN: Is it?
BOY: Yes, and that's Fred. He wants to be a pirate!

[pause]

3

Boy:	There's my new friend, Paul.
Woman:	So he was on this holiday too? That's nice.
Boy:	He's playing in the sand between those two rocks, look!
Woman:	What's he making?
Boy:	A kind of star, I think.

[pause]

4

Woman:	And who's that woman?
Boy:	That's my mum. Her name's Mary.
Woman:	Did she bring you a picnic that day?
Boy:	Yes. And she's got her sun hat on. It was very sunny there.

[pause]

5

Boy:	And Vicky's in this picture too. She's got a drink in her hand. Can you see her?
Woman:	Oh, yes. She's got a dolphin on her T-shirt!
Boy:	That's right. She's another friend of mine. We looked for treasure one day, but we didn't find any!
Woman:	Oh dear!

[pause]

Now listen to Part 1 again.

[The recording is repeated.]

[pause]

That is the end of Part 1.

[pause]

Part 2 *Listen and look. There is one example.*

[pause]

Girl:	Dad? Can I have some dance lessons? We can go to dance lessons at school now.
Man:	I don't know, Daisy.
Girl:	Please? There's a new teacher at school who can dance well.
Man:	Hmm … I don't know.

[pause]

Can you see the answer? Now you listen and write.

[pause]

1

Man:	Tell me about the dance lessons.
Girl:	They aren't in my classroom.
Man:	Which classroom are they in, then?
Girl:	They're in classroom ten. The one next to the playground.
Man:	Classroom ten. OK.

[pause]

2

Man:	And which day are these lessons? Do you know?
Girl:	Yes. They're on Monday.
Man:	On Monday … hmm. That's OK, I think.
Girl:	So can I, Dad?

[pause]

3

Man:	Well, what's the name of the teacher who can give you these lessons?
Girl:	It's Mrs Caris.
Man:	Let me write this down. Mrs Caris: C-A-R-I-S.
Girl:	Yes. She's our English teacher too.
Man:	Oh!

[pause]

4

Girl:	But you have to buy me something.
Man:	What? A new dress?
Girl:	No. Some shoes. We have to take them to the first lesson.
Man:	Do they have to be new shoes?
Girl:	Yes, please!

[pause]

5

Man:	But how can you come home after the lesson? On the bus?
Girl:	No. There isn't a bus then. I can take my bike that day and ride home.
Man:	On your bike – that's a good idea! All right. You can go to the dance lessons.
Girl:	Great!

[pause]

Now listen to Part 2 again.

[The recording is repeated.]

[pause]

That is the end of Part 2.

[pause]

Part 3 *Look at the pictures. What did John do last week?*
Listen and look. There is one example.

[pause]

Woman:	Did you have a good week with your cousin, John?
Boy:	Yes, it was great, Miss White. They live in a big town.
Woman:	Oh, yes? Tell me! What did you do there?
Boy:	We went skating on Wednesday. I enjoyed it a lot.

[pause]

Can you see the line from the word Wednesday? On Wednesday, John went skating.

Now you listen and draw lines.

[pause]

1

BOY:	We had a party another day.
WOMAN:	Which day was that?
BOY:	It was on Friday. It was my cousin's birthday. Her friend gave her a rabbit!
WOMAN:	Wow! And did you give her a present?
BOY:	Yes – a football, but we couldn't play because it rained that day.

[pause]

2

BOY:	We went on a bus one day. We sat upstairs in the front.
WOMAN:	Was that on Monday?
BOY:	No … it was on Thursday morning, I think. Yes, Thursday, that's right.
WOMAN:	And where did you go?
BOY:	To a kind of park. We played games there on the grass.

[pause]

3

BOY:	Sunday was my best day.
WOMAN:	What did you do that day?
BOY:	My aunt got us some tickets and we went to see a film.
WOMAN:	What was it about?
BOY:	A family of rabbits. It was very funny. They could talk!

[pause]

4

WOMAN:	And what did you do on Tuesday, John?
BOY:	On Tuesday? Ermm … that was a quiet day, I think. We were at home that day. I read a book in the living room.
WOMAN:	Was it a good story?
BOY:	It was OK. It was about a rabbit. It wasn't very exciting.

[pause]

5

BOY:	And on Saturday evening, I came home again.
WOMAN:	But what did you do in the day, before that? Did you go into the town again?
BOY:	Not that day. My uncle played football with us and we had a picnic in the garden.
WOMAN:	Great!
BOY:	Yes. I always enjoy my holidays there.

[pause]

Now listen to Part 3 again.

[The recording is repeated.]

[pause]

That is the end of Part 3.

[pause]

Part 4 *Look at the pictures. Listen and look.*

There is one example.

[pause]

What's Tony doing?

[pause]

WOMAN:	Tony! Are you having a bath?
MAN:	No, I'm getting some water to wash the car. Why?
WOMAN:	It's all right. I could hear water, that's all. Do you want a drink? I'm making some tea.
MAN:	No, thank you!

[pause]

Can you see the tick? Now you listen and tick the box.

[pause]

1 What did Jane buy yesterday?

MAN:	What's that, Jane?
GIRL:	It's a cup for Mum. I got it in a big shop.
MAN:	When you went shopping yesterday?
GIRL:	Yes, I took the puppy with me. I had a good day, but I didn't buy any new shoes. I wanted some, but I couldn't find any.
MAN:	Oh!

[pause]

2 What was Jack's dream about?

WOMAN:	Are you all right, Jack?
BOY:	No, Mum. I had a funny dream.
WOMAN:	Was it about monsters again?
BOY:	No, it was about a big bear. I was afraid.
WOMAN:	Well, get up now and come and have some breakfast!

[pause]

3 Where's Peter's mouse?

BOY:	Grandma, I can't find my mouse. He isn't in his cage.
WOMAN:	Oh, Peter! Have you looked in your box? He was there yesterday when you couldn't find him.
BOY:	I looked there. What's that? Look! That sock's moving!
WOMAN:	It's your mouse! He's inside it.
BOY:	Oh, yes! You naughty mouse! Come here!

[pause]

4 Which person is Kim?

GIRL: There's my friend Kim, Dad.
MAN: Do you mean the girl in the red trousers?
GIRL: Not her. I mean the girl in the red skirt. Can you see her?
MAN: The person with the red jacket on too?
GIRL: Dad! That's Kim's mother! Put your glasses on!

[pause]

5 What did Mr Rice find in his car?

WOMAN: Mr Rice is on television, Pat. He's found something in his car. It's very funny.
GIRL: Mum! I'm reading my book about spiders.
WOMAN: Oh … it's a toy fish on the floor of his car! Look!
GIRL: What?
WOMAN: Come and see.
GIRL: No! Please be quiet!

[pause]

Now listen to Part 4 again.

[The recording is repeated.]

[pause]

That is the end of Part 4.

[pause]

Part 5   *Look at the picture. Listen and look.*

There is one example.

[pause]

GIRL: I'd like to colour this picture now. Can I do that?
MAN: Yes, you can. It's a kitchen. Can you see the apple in the boy's hand?
GIRL: Yes. Shall I colour it?
MAN: Yes, please. Colour that apple yellow.
GIRL: OK.

[pause]

Can you see the yellow apple? This is an example.

Now you listen and colour and draw.

[pause]

1

MAN: Now find the two bowls.
GIRL: OK. I can see the two bowls.
MAN: Good. Colour the bigger one, please. Make it blue.
GIRL: OK. I'm colouring it now.
MAN: Good.

[pause]

2

GIRL: There's a doll on the table. Can I colour that too?
MAN: Yes. Good idea!
GIRL: Can I colour it yellow?
MAN: Hmm … no. Make it green.
GIRL: All right. What a funny doll!

[pause]

3

MAN: Now, please draw something in this kitchen.
GIRL: OK. What must I draw? Something easy, please!
MAN: All right! Draw a bottle inside the cupboard. The cupboard with the door that's open.
GIRL: A bottle. OK. I'll do that now.

[pause]

4

GIRL: There are two bags in this room. Shall I colour the square one?
MAN: No. Colour the round bag next.
GIRL: Can I choose the colour? I'd like to colour it pink.
MAN: That's fine.
GIRL: Thank you.

[pause]

5

MAN: Now, outside the window there's a big plant in the garden. Can you see it?
GIRL: Yes. Shall I colour that too?
MAN: Yes, please. Make the big plant purple.
GIRL: OK. That's one of my favourite colours. It looks nice.
MAN: Yes, it does. Thank you!

[pause]

Now listen to Part 5 again.

[The recording is repeated.]

[pause]

That is the end of the Movers Practice Listening Test 2.

Reading and Writing

Part 1 (6 marks)

1 eggs   2 CDs   3 a bat   4 carrots
5 a snake   6 lemons

Part 2 (6 marks)

1 no   2 no   3 yes   4 no   5 no   6 no

Part 3 (6 marks)

1 A   2 C   3 A   4 C   5 B   6 A

Part 4 (7 marks)

1 swim   2 kitchen   3 village   4 talked
5 ride   6 apples   7 Paul's day in the country

Part 5 (10 marks)

1 table tennis   2 Sue(the) girl/daughter
3 (they/the family had) lunch
4 Sue's/his cousin's (bed)room   5 (the) breakfast
6 the zoo   7 Peter(the) boy/cousin
8 (very) surprised   9 (The) elephants   10 café

Part 6 (5 marks)

1 are   2 than   3 in   4 their   5 can

Speaking

Part	Examiner does this:	Examiner says this:	Minimum response expected from child:	Back-up questions:
	Usher brings candidate in.	Usher to examiner: **Hello. This is (child's name)*.**		
		Examiner: **Hello, *. My name's Jane/Ms Smith.**	**Hello.**	
		How old are you, *?	*nine*	**Are you nine/ten?**
1	Points to **Find the differences** pictures.	**Look at these pictures. They look the same, but some things are different. This coat is blue, but this coat is red.**		
		What other different things can you see?	Describes four other differences: • big/small shell • 2 dolphins/1 dolphin • no shoes/shoes • fishing/sleeping	Point to other differences the candidate does not mention. Give first half of response: **This shell is big, but this shell …**
2	Points to **Picture Story.** Allows time to look at the pictures.	**Now look at these pictures. They show a story. It's called 'John and the snow'. Just look at the pictures first. (Pause.) Look at the first one.** **John's happy because it's snowing. Dad's saying, 'Have breakfast, then put on your coat and scarf and you can play in the snow.'**		
		Now you tell the story. (pointing at the other pictures)	(Many variations possible) *John's eating his breakfast quickly.* *John's looking for his hat and scarf.* *John is in the garden but he isn't happy. It isn't snowing now. It's sunny!*	Questions to prompt other parts of the story: **What's John doing now?** **What's he looking for?** **Where's John now? Is John happy? Why not?**

* Remember to use the child's name throughout the test.

Part	Examiner does this:	Examiner says this:	Minimum response expected from child:	Back-up questions:
3	Points to the **Odd-one-out** pictures.	**Now look at these four pictures. One is different. The book is different. A lemon, a pineapple and an orange are fruit. You eat them. You don't eat a book. You read it.**		
	Points to the second, third and fourth set of pictures in turn.	**Now you tell me about these pictures. Which one is different? (Why?)**	Candidate suggests a difference (any plausible difference is acceptable).	**These are all … ?** (shops) **And this is a … ?** (house) **What colour are these?** (pink) **And this?** (blue) **What are these people doing?** (driving) **And this girl?** (riding a horse)
4	Puts away all pictures.	**Now let's talk about hobbies and sports.**		
		When do you play computer games?	*after school*	**Do you play computer games** *after school*?
		What do you like reading?	*comics*	**Do you like reading** *comics*?
		Where do you watch television?	*(in the) living room*	**Do you watch TV** *in the living room*?
		Tell me about your favourite sport.	*It's football.*	**Is your favourite sport** *football*?
			I play with my friends.	**Who do you** *play with*?
		OK, thank you, *. **Goodbye.**	**Goodbye.**	

* Remember to use the child's name throughout the test.

Test 3 Answers

Listening

Part 1 (5 marks)

Lines should be drawn between:

1 Peter and the boy on the bike, waving
2 Lucy and the girl in the blue skirt, with a dog
3 John and the taller boy playing football
4 Anna and the woman with the baby, wearing sunglasses
5 Bill and the boy hiding in a tree, wearing a red sweater

Part 2 (5 marks)

1 (by) car   2 (in the) evening(s)   3 (his) son
4 (the) shower(s) (here/there)   5 38/thirty eight (years (old))

Part 3 (5 marks)

1 Wednesday – climbed a rock on the beach
2 Saturday – walk in the village, ice cream
3 Tuesday – fishing in boat
4 Friday – film about a woman climber
5 Sunday – read book on beach

Part 4 (5 marks)

1 A   2 B   3 C   4 A   5 B

Part 5 (5 marks)

1 Colour the towel on the woman's head – yellow
2 Colour the boy's scarf – brown
3 Draw a cup on the table in the garden
4 Colour the downstairs door – green
5 Colour the star on the window – purple

TRANSCRIPT   *Hello. This is the Cambridge Movers Practice Listening Test, Test 3.*

Part 1   *Look at Part 1. Look at the picture. Listen and look. There is one example.*

[pause]

BOY: I went to the new park yesterday, Grandma, and took a photo. Look!
WOMAN: Oh, yes! Who's the boy who's wearing jeans and playing with the kite?
BOY: That's my friend, Tony. He's in my class.
WOMAN: Is he?
BOY: Yes. I often play with him.

[pause]

Can you see the line? This is an example. Now you listen and draw lines.

[pause]

1

BOY: Look, there's Peter. That's his new bike.
WOMAN: Wow! Did he get that for his birthday last week?
BOY: Yes. He's waving. Can you see?
WOMAN: Yes.

[pause]

2

BOY: And the girl with the dog ... she's wearing a blue skirt. She's in my class too.
WOMAN: Oh! What's her name?
BOY: It's Lucy.
WOMAN: Does she live near the park?
BOY: I don't know.

[pause]

3

WOMAN: Look at the two boys who are playing with the football. Are they your friends too?
BOY: One of them is – the taller one.

19

WOMAN: And what's his name?
BOY: John. I think the other boy is his brother.
WOMAN: I see.

[pause]

4

WOMAN: And who's this person – the woman with the baby?
BOY: Oh, that's my mum's friend, Anna. She likes going for walks in the park.
WOMAN: She's wearing sunglasses.
BOY: Yes. It was a nice day.

[pause]

5

BOY: There's Bill. He's wearing a red sweater. Can you see?
WOMAN: No.
BOY: Look! In the tree. He's hiding.
WOMAN: What a naughty boy!
BOY: He isn't naughty. He's funny!

[pause]

Now listen to Part 1 again.

[The recording is repeated.]

[pause]

That is the end of Part 1.

[pause]

Part 2   *Listen and look. There is one example.*

[pause]

GIRL: Excuse me, Pat! Can I ask you some questions? It's about this sports centre.
MAN: Yes! What kind of questions?
GIRL: It's for my homework. Which sport do you play here?
MAN: Tennis.
GIRL: Tennis, OK. Thanks.

[pause]

Can you see the answer? Now you listen and write.

[pause]

1

GIRL: And when you come, do you drive here?
MAN: Yes. It's quicker and easier for us.
GIRL: So, you come in your car?
MAN: Yes, that's right.

[pause]

2

GIRL: When do you come here to the sports centre?
MAN: I come here in the evenings.
GIRL: Not in the afternoons?
MAN: No. I'm at work then.

[pause]

3

GIRL: And do you come here with your friends?
MAN: No, not with my friends, with my son.
GIRL: With your son? Oh, where is he now?
MAN: He went to buy a bottle of water.

[pause]

4

GIRL: And what don't you like about the sports centre?
MAN: I think it's all OK.
GIRL: Oh?
MAN: Well … I don't like the showers here.
GIRL: The showers. You don't like those, OK.
MAN: No, I don't.

[pause]

5

GIRL: And my last question. How old are you?
MAN: I'm 38.
GIRL: Sorry? 38?
MAN: Yes.
GIRL: OK. Thank you.

[pause]

Now listen to Part 2 again.

[The recording is repeated.]

[pause]

That is the end of Part 2.

[pause]

Part 3   *Look at the pictures. What did Ben do last week? Listen and look. There is one example.*

[pause]

WOMAN: Did you have a good week by the sea, Ben?
BOY: It was OK, Grandma, but the weather wasn't very good.
WOMAN: Oh dear! Well, what did you do on Monday?
BOY: We went to a kind of museum and saw lots of different fish.

[pause]

Can you see the line from the word Monday? On Monday, Ben went to see some fish. Now you listen and draw lines.

[pause]

1

BOY: Wednesday was good. It wasn't cold that day.
WOMAN: Great. What did you do that day?
BOY: We went to the beach and climbed up to the top of a big rock.
WOMAN: Oh! Were you afraid?
BOY: No. But it was very difficult to climb.

[pause]

2

WOMAN: But what did you do on the first day, on Saturday?
BOY: We went for a walk in the village.
WOMAN: Was it good there?
BOY: Yes. There were lots of small shops and Dad bought us ice creams!

[pause]

3

BOY: But Tuesday was very boring.
WOMAN: Tuesday?
BOY: Yes. Dad wanted to go fishing from a boat and I went with him.
WOMAN: How many fish did you catch?
BOY: We didn't catch any! It was windy and cold again. I didn't enjoy that afternoon.

[pause]

4

BOY: On Thursday, we went to the cinema. No, sorry, that was Friday.
WOMAN: And which film did you see?
BOY: It was about a woman who did something exciting.
WOMAN: Why? What did she do?
BOY: She climbed a mountain.
WOMAN: Wow! That is exciting.

[pause]

5

WOMAN: The weather was great on Sunday. Did you go in a boat then?
BOY: No, but we went to the beach.
WOMAN: What did you do there?
BOY: Well, I bought a book in the village shop and I sat on the sand and read it.
WOMAN: What was the story about?
BOY: A boy who goes on a holiday to the beach!

[pause]

Now listen to Part 3 again.

[The recording is repeated.]

[pause]

That is the end of Part 3.

[pause]

Part 4   *Look at the pictures. Listen and look.*

There is one example.

[pause]

What's Mary doing?

[pause]

WOMAN: Mary! What are you doing? Are you watching television again?
GIRL: No, Mum, I'm cleaning my bedroom.
WOMAN: Good! And did you phone Grandpa this morning?

GIRL: Yes. I did that after breakfast.

[pause]

Can you see the tick? Now you listen and tick the box.

[pause]

1 Where did Alex walk to today?

MAN: Did you take the dog for a walk to the river today, Alex?
GIRL: Not today, Dad. It rained and rained. I didn't want to go for a long walk.
MAN: Did you go to the playground, then?
GIRL: No. We only walked to the apartments at the end of the street. Then we came home again!

[pause]

2 What has Jack got for lunch today?

MAN: I had a terrible lunch at work yesterday. I bought a burger. It looked good, but I didn't enjoy it.
WOMAN: Well, I'm making a salad for you today, Jack.
MAN: That's my favourite, thanks.
WOMAN: Do you like vegetable soup? I can make some of that for you on Saturday.
MAN: OK.

[pause]

3 What kind of pet does Fred have?

WOMAN: We're talking about pets today, children. Do you have a pet at home, Fred?
BOY: Yes, Miss Last. I've got a kitten. It likes watching the birds in our garden!
WOMAN: Does it?
BOY: Yes, and my brother's got a mouse, but I never play with it.
WOMAN: Oh.

[pause]

4 Which girl is Daisy?

GIRL: You know my friend Daisy, Dad?
MAN: The girl with the long, curly hair?
GIRL: No, she's got short hair now. And it isn't curly. I want my hair like that.
MAN: Why do you want yours like that?
GIRL: I want to be like Daisy!

[pause]

5 What's the weather like at Jane's house today?

GIRL: Hello, Aunt Sally! How are you?
WOMAN: Oh, hello, Jane. I'm fine, thank you. It's a nice, sunny day here!
GIRL: That's good! It's raining here in our town.
WOMAN: Oh, that's sad. It snowed here yesterday. The ground's all white outside.
GIRL: Wow!

[pause]

Now listen to Part 4 again.

[The recording is repeated.]

[pause]

That is the end of Part 4.

[pause]

Part 5 *Look at the picture. Listen and look.*

There is one example.

[pause]

MAN: Would you like to colour this picture now? Can you see the cat?

GIRL: The one on the balcony? Yes! It's got a very long tail!

MAN: That's right. Colour that cat pink for me, please.

GIRL: All right.

[pause]

Can you see the pink cat? This is an example.

Now you listen and colour and draw.

[pause]

1

MAN: Now, can you see the woman in the bathroom?

GIRL: Yes, but why has she got a towel on her head?

MAN: Because her hair's wet. Colour that towel for me. Make it yellow.

GIRL: OK. I'm doing it now.

MAN: Good.

[pause]

2

GIRL: Can I colour the boy's scarf too?

MAN: The scarf that the boy is wearing?

GIRL: Yes. Can I colour it brown, please?

MAN: Hmm … Yes! Good idea!

[pause]

3

MAN: Now, would you like to draw something on this picture too?

GIRL: Yes! I like drawing.

MAN: Good. Then draw a cup on the table in the garden.

GIRL: A cup? On the table?

MAN: Yes, please.

[pause]

4

GIRL: The girl is opening the door. Can I colour that now too?

MAN: Yes. What colour?

GIRL: Hmm … I don't know. How about green?

MAN: OK. That's a good colour for a door.

[pause]

5

MAN: Now, can you see the star?

GIRL: Which one? The one in the window?

MAN: That's right. Colour that star for me now. Make it purple.

GIRL: All right. I like this picture now.

Man: Me too!

[pause]

Now listen to Part 5 again.

[The recording is repeated.]

[pause]

That is the end of the Movers Practice Listening Test 3.

Reading and Writing

Part 1 (6 marks)

1 comics   2 teeth   3 plants   4 DVDs
5 a shoulder   6 forests

Part 2 (6 marks)

1 no   2 yes   3 yes   4 no   5 no   6 no

Part 3 (6 marks)

1 B   2 C   3 A   4 B   5 C   6 A

Part 4 (7 marks)

1 sunny   2 cup   3 shouted   4 nurse
5 carrots   6 hop   7 Skip isn't well

Part 5 (10 marks)

1 train   2 panda (bear)   3 Sally   4 giraffes
5 scarf   6 took a photo(graph)/picture
7 (the) dolphins   8 ball   9 (all) wet   10 coat

Part 6 (5 marks)

1 do   2 or   3 them   4 of   5 who

Speaking

Part	Examiner does this:	Examiner says this:	Minimum response expected from child:	Back-up questions:
	Usher brings candidate in.	Usher to examiner: **Hello, this is (*child's name*)*.** Examiner: **Hello, *. My name's *Jane/Ms Smith*.** **How old are you, *?**	**Hello.** *nine*	 Are you *nine/ten*?
1	Points to **Find the differences** pictures.	**Look at these pictures. They look the same, but some things are different. This woman has fair hair, but this woman has black hair.** **What other different things can you see?**	 Describes four other differences: • picture of lake/ mountains • 1 ruler/2 rulers • raining/not raining • handbag under/on table	 Point to other differences the candidate does not mention. Give first half of response: **Here there's a picture of a lake, but here …**
2	Points to **Picture Story.** Allows time to look at the pictures.	**Now look at these pictures. They show a story. It's called 'Sally's presents'. Just look at the pictures first. (Pause.) Look at the first one.** **It's Sally's birthday. Her parents and her brother are giving her presents. Sally wants a new computer game!** **Now you tell the story.** (pointing at the other pictures)	 (Many variations possible) *Sally's opening the present. It's a guitar! Sally's very unhappy. She doesn't want a guitar.* *Now Sally's opening the present from her brother. It's a computer game. She's happy now.* *Sally and her brother are playing with the new computer game. Dad's playing the guitar.*	 Questions to prompt other parts of the story: **What's Sally's present from her parents?** **Is Sally happy?** **What's Sally doing now?** **What's the present?** **What are Sally and her brother doing?** **What's her dad doing?**

* Remember to use the child's name throughout the test.

Part	Examiner does this:	Examiner says this:	Minimum response expected from child:	Back-up questions:
3	Points to **Odd-one-out** pictures.	**Now look at these four pictures. One is different. The book is different. A lemon, a pineapple and an orange are fruit. You eat them. You don't eat a book. You read it.**		
	Points to the second, third and fourth sets of pictures in turn.	**Now you tell me about these pictures. Which one is different? (Why?)**	Candidate suggests a difference (any plausible difference is acceptable).	**Where do these live?** (water) **And this?** (jungle) **What are these?** (clothes) **And this?** (toy) **What are these people doing?** (reading) **And this girl?** (skating)
4	Puts away all pictures.	**Now let's talk about food.**		
		What's your favourite food?	*chips/fries*	**Do you like *chips/fries*?**
		Who cooks the food in your family?	*my mother*	**Does your *mother* cook the food in your family?**
		Where do you eat in your home?	*(in the) kitchen*	**Do you eat *in the kitchen*?**
		Tell me about your breakfast.	*I eat bread.* *I drink orange juice.*	**Do you eat *bread*?** **Do you drink *orange juice*?**
		OK, thank you, *. **Goodbye.**	Goodbye.	

* Remember to use the child's name throughout the test.

COMBINED STARTERS AND MOVERS THEMATIC VOCABULARY LIST

For ease of reference, vocabulary is arranged in semantic groups or themes. Some words appear under more than one heading.

In addition to the topics, notions and concepts listed for the syllabus, the following categories appear:

- useful words and expressions
- adjectives
- pronouns
- determiners
- verbs
- adverbs
- modals
- prepositions
- question words
- conjunctions
- names

s – first appears at *Starters*
m – first appears at *Movers*

ANIMALS

s animal
m bat
m bear
s bird
m cage
s cat
s chicken
s cow
s crocodile
s dog
m dolphin
s duck
s elephant
s fish (s & pl)
m fly
s frog
s giraffe
s goat
s hippo
s horse
m jungle
m kangaroo
m kitten
m lion
s lizard
s monkey
s mouse/mice
m panda
m parrot
m pet
m puppy
m rabbit
m shark
s sheep (s & pl)
s snake
s spider
s tail
s tiger
m whale
s zoo

THE BODY & FACE

s arm
m back
m beard
m blond(e)
s body
m curly
s ear
s eye
s face
m fair
m fat
s foot/feet
s hair
s hand
s head
s leg
m moustache
s mouth
m neck
s nose
m shoulder
s smile
m stomach
m straight
m thin
m tooth/teeth

CLOTHES

s bag
s clothes
m coat
s dress
s glasses
s handbag
s hat
s jacket
s jeans
m scarf
s shirt
s shoe
s skirt
s sock
m sweater
s trousers
s T-shirt
s watch
s wear

COLOURS

s black
s blue
s brown
s colour
s green
s grey (US gray)
s orange
s pink
s purple
s red
s white
s yellow

FAMILY & FRIENDS

m aunt
s baby
s boy
s brother
s child/children
s cousin
s dad(dy)
m daughter
s family
s father
s friend
s girl
m grandchild(ren)
m granddaughter
s grandfather
s grandma
s grandmother
s grandpa
m grandparent
m grandson
m grown-up
s live
s man/men
s Miss
s mother
s Mr
s Mrs
s mum(my) (US mom(my))
s old
m parent
s person/people
s sister
m son
s their
s them
s they
m uncle
s us
s we
s woman/women
s you
s your
s young

FOOD & DRINK

s apple
s banana
s bean
m bottle
m bowl
s bread
s breakfast
s burger
s cake
s candy (UK sweets)

s carrot
m cheese
s chicken
s chips (US fries)
s chocolate
s coconut
m coffee
m cup
s dinner
s drink (n & v)
s eat
s egg
s fish
s food
s fries (UK chips)
s fruit
m glass (of)
s grape
m hungry
s ice cream
s juice
s lemon
s lemonade
s lime
s lunch
s mango
s meat
s milk
s onion
s orange
m pasta
s pea
s pear
m picnic
s pineapple
m plate
s potato
s rice
m salad
m sandwich
s sausage
m soup
s supper
s sweet(s) (US candy)
m tea
m thirsty
s tomato
m vegetable
s water
s watermelon

HEALTH

m cold
m cough
m cry
m doctor
m earache

m fall
m fine
m headache
m hospital
m hurt
m matter (What's the matter?)
m nurse
m stomach-ache
m temperature
m tired
m toothache

THE HOME

m address
s apartment (UK flat)
s armchair
m balcony
m basement
s bath
s bathroom
s bed
s bedroom
m blanket
s bookcase
s box
s camera
m CD player
s chair
s clock
s computer
s cupboard
s desk
s dining room
s doll
s door
m downstairs
m dream
m DVD player
m elevator (UK lift)
m fan
s flat (US apartment)
s floor
m floor (ground, 1st, etc.)
s flower
s garden
s hall
s home
s house
m internet
s kitchen
s lamp
m lift (US elevator)
s living room
s mat
m message
s mirror
s painting

s phone
s picture
s radio
m roof
s room
m seat
m shopping
m shower
s sleep
s sofa
m stair(s)
s table
s television/TV
m toothbrush
m towel
s toy
s tree
m upstairs
s wall
m wash (n & v)
s watch
s window

NUMBERS

s Cardinals: 1–20
m Cardinals: 21–100
m hundred
m Ordinals: 1st–20th
m pair

PLACES & DIRECTIONS

m above
m bank
s behind
m below
s between
s bookshop
m bus station
m bus stop
m café
m centre
m cinema
m circle
m city/town centre
m farm
s here
m hospital
s in
s in front of
m library
m map
m market
m near
s next to
s on
m opposite

s park
m place
s playground
m road
s shop (US store)
m sports centre
m square
m station
s store (UK shop)
m straight
s street
m supermarket
m swimming pool
s there
m town/city centre
s under
s zoo

SCHOOL

s alphabet
s answer
s ask
s board
s book
s bookcase
m break
s class
s classroom
s close
s colour
s computer
s correct
s cross
s cupboard
s desk
s door
s draw(ing)
s English
s eraser (UK rubber)
s example
s find
s floor
m homework
m internet
s keyboard (computer)
s know
s learn
s lesson
s letter (as in alphabet)
s line
s listen (to)
s look
m mistake
s mouse (computer)
s music
s name
s number

s open
s page
s part
s pen
s pencil
s picture
s playground
s question
s read
s right (as in correct)
s rubber (US eraser)
s ruler
s school
s sentence
s sit
s spell
s stand (up)
s story
s teacher
s tell
s test (n & v)
m text
s tick (n & v)
s understand
s wall
m website
s window
s word
s write

SPORTS & LEISURE

s badminton
s ball
m band (music)
s baseball
s basketball
m bat
s beach
s bike
s boat
s book
s bounce
s camera
s catch
m CD
m CD player
m comic/comic book
m dance
s doll
s draw(ing)
m drive (n)
s drive (v)
m DVD
m DVD player
m email
s enjoy
s favourite

m film (US movie)
m fish (v)
s fish(ing)
s fly
s football (US soccer)
s game
m go shopping
s guitar
s hit
s hobby
s hockey
m holiday
m hop
s jump
m kick (n)
s kick (v)
s kite
s listen (to)
m movie (UK film)
s music
s paint(ing)
m party
s photo
s piano
s picture
s play (with)
m present
s radio
s read
m ride (n)
s ride (v)
s run
m sail
s sing
m skate
m skip
s soccer (UK football)
s song
s sport
m sports centre
s story
m swim (n)
m swimming pool
s table tennis
s take a photo/picture
s television/TV
s tennis
m text
s throw
m towel
s toy
s TV/television
m video
m walk (n)
s walk (v)
s watch

TIME

m after
s afternoon
m age
m always
m before
s birthday
s clock
s day
s end
s evening
m every
s morning
m never
s night
m sometimes
s today
s watch
m week
m weekend
s year
m yesterday
  The days of the week:
m Sunday
m Monday
m Tuesday
m Wednesday
m Thursday
m Friday
m Saturday

TOYS

s alien
s ball
s balloon
s baseball
s basketball
s bike
s boat
s car
s doll
s football (US soccer)
s game
s helicopter
s kite
s lorry (US truck)
s monster
s plane
s robot
s soccer (UK football)
s toy
s train
m treasure
s truck (UK lorry)

TRANSPORT

s bike
s boat
s bus
m bus station
m bus stop
s car
m drive (n)
s drive (v)
m driver
s fly (v)
s go
s helicopter
s lorry (US truck)
s motorbike
s plane
m ride (n)
s ride (v)
s run
m station
s swim
m ticket
s train
m trip
s truck (UK lorry)
m walk (n)
s walk (v)

WEATHER

m cloud
m cloudy
m rain
m rainbow
m snow
s sun
m sunny
m weather
m wind
m windy

WORK

m clown
m doctor
m driver
m farmer
m hospital
m nurse
m pirate
s teacher
m work

THE WORLD AROUND US

s beach
m city
m country(side)
m field

m forest
m grass
m ground
m island
m jungle
m lake
m leaf/leaves
m moon
m mountain
m plant
m river
m road
m rock
s sand
s sea
s shell
m star
s street
s sun
m town
s tree
m village
s water
m waterfall
m world

USEFUL WORDS & EXPRESSIONS

s bye (-bye)
m come on!
m excuse me
s goodbye
s hello
s I don't know
s no
s oh
s oh dear
s OK
s pardon
s please
s right
m see you!
s so
s sorry
s thank you
s thanks
s then
s well
s well done
s wow!
s yes

ADJECTIVES

m afraid
m all
m all right
s angry

m awake
m back
m bad
s beautiful
m best
m better
s big
m blond(e)
m boring
m bottom
m busy
m careful
s clean
m clever
s closed
m cloudy
m cold
s correct
m curly
m different
m difficult
s dirty
s double
m dry
m easy
s English
m every
m exciting
m fair
m famous
m fat
s favourite
m fine
m first
m frightened
s funny
s good
s great
s happy
s her
s his
m hot
m hungry
s its
m last
s long
m loud
m more
m most
s my
m naughty
s new
s nice
s OK
s old
s open
s our
m pretty

m quick
m quiet
s right (correct)
m round
s sad
m safe
m second
s short
m slow
s small
s sorry
m square
m straight
m strong
m sunny
m surprised
m sweet
m tall
m terrible
s their
m thin
m third
m thirsty
m tired
m top
s ugly
m weak
m well
m wet
m windy
m worse
m worst
m wrong
s young
s your

DETERMINERS

s a/an
s a lot of
m all
m another
m any
m both
m every
s lots of
s many
m more
m most
s no
s one
s some
s that
s the
s these
s this
s those

ADVERBS

s   a lot
s   again
m   all
m   all right
m   always
m   back
m   badly
m   best
m   better
m   carefully
m   down
m   downstairs
m   first
s   here
s   home
m   how
m   how much
m   how often
m   inside
m   last
s   lots
m   loudly
m   more
m   most
m   near
m   never
s   no
s   not
s   now
m   off
m   often
m   on
m   only
m   out
m   outside
m   quickly
m   quietly
s   really
m   round
m   second
m   slowly
m   sometimes
m   then
s   there
m   third
s   today
s   too
m   up
m   upstairs
s   very
m   well
m   when
m   worse
m   worst
s   yes
m   yesterday

PREPOSITIONS

s   about
m   above
m   after
s   at (prep of place)
m   at (prep of time)
m   before
s   behind
m   below
s   between
m   by
m   down
s   for
s   from
s   in (prep of place)
m   in (prep of time)
s   in front of
m   inside
m   into
s   like
m   near
s   next to
s   of
m   off
s   on (prep of place)
m   on (prep of time)
m   opposite
m   out of
m   outside
m   round
m   than
s   to
s   under
m   up
s   with

CONJUNCTIONS

s   and
m   because
s   but
s   or
m   than
m   when

PRONOUNS

s   a lot
m   all
m   another
m   any
m   both
m   everyone
m   everything
s   he
s   her
s   hers
s   him

s   his
s   I
s   it
s   its
s   lots
s   me
s   mine
m   more
m   most
m   nothing
s   one
s   ours
s   she
m   someone
m   something
s   that
s   theirs
s   them
s   these
s   they
s   this
s   those
s   us
s   we
m   which
m   who
s   you
s   yours

VERBS

Irregular:

s   be
m   be called
m   bring
m   buy
s   catch (a ball)
m   catch (a bus)
s   choose
s   come
s   do
s   draw
s   drink
s   drive
m   dry
s   eat
m   fall
s   find
s   fly
s   get
m   get (un)dressed
m   get (up/on/off)
s   give
s   go
m   go shopping
s   have
s   have (got)

m have (got) to
m hide
s hit
s hold
m hurt
s know
s learn
s let's
m lose
s make
m mean
s put
m put on
s read
s ride
s run
s say
s see
s sing
s sit (down)
s sleep
s spell
s stand (up)
s swim
m take
m take (a bus)
s take (a photo)
m take off
s tell
m think
s throw
s understand
m wake up
s wear
s write

Regular:
s add
s answer
s ask
s bounce
m call
m carry
m change
s clean
m climb
s close
s colour
s complete
m cook
s cross
m cry
m dance
m dream
m dress up
m drop
m email
s enjoy

m film
m fish
m help
m hop
m invite
s jump
s kick
m laugh
s learn
s like
s listen (to)
s live
s look
s look (at)
m look for
s love
m move
m need
s open
s paint
s phone
s pick up
m plant
s play (with)
s point
m rain
m sail
m shop
m shout
s show
m skate
m skip
s smile
m snow
s start
s stop
s talk
s test
m text
s tick
m travel
s try
m video
m wait
s walk
s want
m wash
s watch
s wave
m work

MODALS

s can/cannot/can't
m could (for ability)
m must
m shall
m would

QUESTION WORDS

s how
s how many
m how much
m how often
s how old
s what
m when
s where
s which
s who
s whose
m why

NAMES

s Alex
s Ann
s Anna
s Ben
s Bill
m Charlie
m Daisy
s Dan
m Fred
s Grace
m Jack
m Jane
s Jill
m Jim
m John
s Kim
m Lily
s Lucy
m Mary
s May
s Nick
s Pat
m Paul
m Peter
m Sally
s Sam
s Sue
s Tom
s Tony
m Vicky